Word Dancing: Instant Poetry (Just add words!) volume 3.

By

"Laughing" Larry Berger

ISBN: 978-81-19228-77-5

First Edition: 2023

Rs. 200/-

Cyberwit.net

HIG 45 Kaushambi Kunj, Kalindipuram

Allahabad - 211011 (U.P.) India

http://www.cyberwit.net

Tel: +(91) 9415091004

E-mail: info@cyberwit.net

Printed at VCORRE PRESS.

Table of Contents

Life Happens

Breathing is an addiction!
Most humans on the planet
crave oxygen and can't wait for the next fix.

And yet,
we drive bigger and bigger cars
cut down even more trees than ever before
conservationist "tree- hugger's" had their say!

The ozone layer is shrinking by the day
and Hydrofracking is poisoning the water!

We now get our fix from portable oxygen tanks
with tubes coming out of our noses and
mouths.
We pass this addiction on to our children

I often wonder:

do we really expect to have a viable recovery
plan

and wean humans away from their breathing
addiction before the next
generation are grown.

A rhyming children's story

There once was a young girl named Sally

who just loved to count and tally.

Whatever she saw she could accurately draw

and soon she was known all over the valley.

One day while at school her teach thought it would be cool

for Sally to speak on her gifts.

She got up from her chair, everyone stared and made Sally feel like a fool.

She hemmed and she hawed

The other kids guffawed

at the way Sally was struggling through.

The teacher said, "For now we'll let it pass but see me after class."

Sally was teary eyed and bawled.

After the bell rang and the kids had left

Sally went up to the teacher's desk

"I'm not going to yell, you actually did rather well!

But I'm concerned about what you felt.

Through her tears Sally related

that she felt hated

by everyone she'd ever called friend

The teacher said "ug!" and gave her a hug

and said everything would work out in the end.

Looking for Answers

Things have gotten weird this year

Everyone's looking for someone to blame.

The Republicans

The Democrats

Where are the Americans?

The Doctors get lost

as people die

We need more people to wear masks

and leave the open road to stay home.

Years ago, it was simple:

Put people in showers

Release the gas

Remove the bodies

Simple.

Now

Get the vaccine

Don't get the vaccine

Where a mask?

Times change

Or do they?

About Driving:

The cars get closer every time

forget the freeways

you're taking your life in your hands

with every movement of the pistons.

Twenty years

That's how long it took for me

to sufficiently recover from watching the last car

I owned blow up in my face and

get behind the wheel.

Twenty years

just like Odysseus after the fall of Troy

they made him myth and legend

maybe they'll do the same for me.

Corned beef and Cabbage

It isn't easy being Green!

Or Orange for that matter!

There is a pot of gold at the end of the rainbow

So why not the rainbow coalition?

"When Irish eyes are smiling…"

We dance to the same tune

Irish Spring

Indian Summer

Nuclear Winter

It's been a busy

Year.

Don’s little fountain

The sun sets
the wind brings
the voices to our ears
as a chorus of friends
sing through the night

Music cascades
through the either
to find its way into our hearts

Magic happens when we share.

For those who knew him

He started as a troublemaker, born to be wild!

Living on coffee, anchovy paste and baked goods.

He learned to trudge through the snows of winter in Rochester New York and learned to fly with Hyland aircraft and even taught others to soar. The military took him, and he scared away the enemy and was only in the Korean war for a day.

I met him in 1966, on a cold October night, a birthday present for his father, a grandson to carry on the name.

Fifty years later

A frail old man

I lift him in my arms to keep him on the bed. He's down to a lifetime low of 118 lbs. From an average of 185 Lbs.

The mass has prevented him from eating for two months but now he can barely speak. The ambulance came to take him in. Two hours later I pick up my mother at the hospital. I say goodbye to him, and we leave.

The next morning and my mother wakes me up to tell me he's dead and my brother is on the way. My mother meets my brother at the hospital. We go for breakfast. Meet with funeral director.

It's hard to sum up a life in a few lines. But I tried!

Rest in peace Poppy!

Grasshopper Girls

(For Kitty J.)

She said:

It's cold in Chicago!

My heart is from Hungary!

Summer is over.

She said:

The baby was just born!

The woods are scary!

Help Me!

They said:

LISTEN TO US!

New year, new rules

We've all got to make a living some how

the bills got to get paid and not just in

beer and pizza!

Home may be a park bench but at least it’s dry

compared to the snowbank next door.

Poets should not have to die to become great

musicians neither

yet who can argue with
Graceland or Dollywood?

Hey, it just dawned on me!

Dolly Parton IS still alive!

I guess some of the great
ones do make it while
they're breathing!

My resolution for the new
year is to do the same.

Snapshot

What do you see when you look into my eyes?

Are you hypnotized by my strength?

Bedazzled by my rugged handsomeness?

Or do you think the photographer was just trying to make sure

his camera worked when he took the shot for the reel picture?

They say that a photograph captures the soul of the subject.

Do you see my soul here? Or do you see me at all?

I'm told I look like Dali, Hitler, the plumber or the handyman.

Do you see me?

Or do you see life etched upon a face?

A mirror for your own mortality.

What do you see in this Photo?

That's the real question huh?

The world is my litter box

Hey all you crazy Kats!

The Kittens are in heat and it’s time to strut.

Toms got the key so let's make the night.

We’re unstoppable now

Plenty of mice and nip!

Lap up the milk and let’s blow this pop stand.

A poem inspired by the movies.

The classics are the best!

Modern action adventure

is Marvelous but the Wizard has left OZ.

Politics and the movies have always been fun

JFK was a hit

Star Wars became the biggest franchise of its day

Let's go back to the future!

All hail the drive in!

Popcorn anyone?

In memory of Yvonne de La Vega

Music flows like a smoky torch

burning time like fireflies

the light flickers in the dark as the Blue Star moves across the Galaxy.

trumpets blast out jazz

the people dance in the streets

as tamales sizzle in the moonlight

and the wine flows

You will be missed

Latina warrior

the word's loss

will echo in my dreams.

Be careful what you wish for

I bought a computer
On it my mom likes to play
But I use if for work
and I don't have a say.

I taught her how to use it
so, I cannot call a halt
to her Facebook jaunts
they really are my fault.

It has brought us closer
and if she has trouble as she cavorts
she lovingly yells at the top of her lungs

"LARRY! I NEED TECH SUPPORT!"

Tree Stand

The roots are the most important
nourishing the body through the core
terminating with the sky

She leaps into downward dog
as she tries to embrace
the sun

Her arms unfolded
she finds her branches empty
as fruit hangs from her twigs

The sun is setting
her leaves fall
and she jogs home.

Word storm

The ink drips from my pen like water

the ink stains the page with tears

as I write these words.

The force of language rumbles through like a hurricane

on Market Street and the birds don't fly that far south no more!

But back in the day

You could hear his horn all the way clear to New York and back to LA again cause baby,

Bird knew how to write on the hearts and minds of those generations yet unborn

Shouting out

Calling them to their future.

And now

The man is dust

And I find these words echo his music and the words just keep dripping from my pen as the notes of his horn play on!

This poem may not be more than a whispering tribute, but the words drip from my pen like water and maybe someday they will bleed like rain.

CLOTHES

Words weave into

Webs of warmth and love.

Sometimes they turn cold like the dead of winter

and can only be fanned to flame through being nailed down and set free.

The diaper and the shroud are the same!

Both cover what is considered unseemly in our eyes

and causes us to close them.

Open your eyes to the current fashion!

See the streets painted red with the clothes of the dead.

Sometimes words matter

Magnificently preparing for the love of the littleness of life

Ants have Families too

Young to care for

dead to bury

and gods to worship.

Whales sing in the deep

joy

sorrow

pain

pleasure

Coral swims with each passing wave

But dies when the sea is calm

Man wanders the earth

One of billions in the night sky

He finds friends with people he never knew existed.

Busy

Lockdown is slowly ending

the caterpillars are emerging from their cocoons

a lot of them

two point five million are already back to work

There is a wall around the White House now

There is marching in the streets

People are participating in that all-American pastime

Protesting

Social distancing is out the window

No one in the crowd is wearing masks

But the message is finally being heard

Look out world!

America is busy!

Timeless

Days pass and things change

First the Gutenberg press,

Now, eBooks and the internet.

Facebook is the first company

in three hundred years

to literally start a revolution,

the first one in history that

no one actually go killed!

People not old enough to vote

can't remember a time when Facebook didn't exist!

It used to take a generation to effect such change.

Now seconds are enough.

Man, I feel old!

Reply for a Goddess

You offer me a treasure far beyond
the dreams of mortal men.

Just one single night with you
Could satisfy the eternal lust
of Zeus himself!
But alas,
I am only a man.
with naught but
Human emotions
Frailties
and I could never worship you as you truly deserve.
All I would ever have to offer you would be my heart.
but how can I possibly give you
That which you already own.

Warriors of the sun

Shields dancing

rays poised,

bows at the ready

they fight for glory and honor.

Years later,

their glow diminished,

they fight once more.

This time for the aid promised them.

Bullets and Grenades have replaced spears and shields.

now the glow leaves more quickly, and the aid is

need sooner.

They all line up,

black dots on the horizon,

One after another,

They beg for a future in which they have a chance to shine.

The moon is rising over the Cemetery.

The Warriors of the sun will shine forever!

One line is all I have.

One line is all I have,

One line, and one line only.

It only takes one line to catch a fish.

It's only the bottom line that matters in

business these days.

Set a course for the future!

I'll follow my one line till it ends

or there are,

no more words!

A Hymn for the church of the big bad doughnut

In the beginning
there was the word
and the word was good.

However,
Man does not live
by bread alone!
And so
T'was created,
The holy bagel.

But man did sin against this
divine creation,

And divided the bagel into
man and woman,

Bella Luna offered of herself
to heal her human cousins.

Please allow me at this time to
correct a misnomer:

The moon is not now,

Nor has it ever been made of

Green cheese!

It is made of Cream Cheese!

But again,

Man did sin,

For he forced love into the
Apple that was forbidden

and floated it away on a river
of tears.

And then he came!

Excuse me a minute.

Sorry! But when I get to this
point in this piece

I hear the voice of the Apostle,
John D. Scone.

He tells me that I will offend
the Biscotti.
and I best change my tone.

But I can't help it!
I have found glazed
and I'm glad!
Have yourself a chocolate
dipped old fashioned
It will be the best you'll every
have!
Come get hip

Have a French twist!

Have yourself a cruller

If you like of that ilk.

Enjoy yourself

A cake made of butter milk!

Come join me if you will

Let's all get cream filled!

Now I've preached the word

and now that you know it

you can say you heard a new Hymn

Brought to you by the church of the big bad doughnut!

Top Banana

Coffee houses hold open mics across the country

that give artists a voice.

Vaudeville is not dead!

The old techniques become new again as time passes.

Vaudeville is not dead!

Festivals and showcases abound.

Vaudeville is not dead!

Grab a cane for a new buck and wing.

Vaudeville is not dead!

Break a leg folks!

Rockstar 2

She comes out of the valley

on nightingale wings.

Hair of flame

Soul of Ice

Her heart warms to the
evening's adventure.

a butterfly

emerging from a cocoon

she walks on stage,

frail and meek and then she
steps up to the mic.

Her voice is guttural,

Smoky and enticing.

What she sings almost doesn't
matter.

But her words are her own.
Her heart beats,
thunder from the mountains
her small chest rises and falls
with the beat.

The breath in her lungs is
visible from the back of the
room as the stage lights are
small suns washing out the
sparkle in her eyes.

Still, she sings.
She sings for all the heartache
she has been through.

She sings her rebirth.
in a new love.

One that is not returned the
way she would like.

And still she sings.

Calling the Jokerman to dance.

Rest and Digest

The day has flown.
You've won!
You made it to get,
where you can be safe!

But you push on,
because there is nothing else
you can do.

You pay as you go but you
miss something,
There is the other side to fight
or flight.

When the lion gets the deer,
They drag it under the nearest tree,
and the Pride joins the hunter.
for the feast.

When the deer gets
away, it goes into the forest,
finds a clear spot with lots of cover,
lays down and shivers till it falls asleep.
Likewise,

humans need to rest and
digest!

It's not just the tryptophan that
causes, the "food comas" of
Thanksgiving!

We need to rest more than
once a year!

family and friends can help,
though

We each need to be our own
health coach.

Nighty night everyone!

Singin in the cold- 1/10/2021

Help, I need somebody!

So, I can roll with the changes.

All you need is love.

It's a miracle.

It is heaven on earth.

with an onion slice!

The weather outside is
frightful.

Please, no more fires!

However, it's always been
burning,

As the world been turning.

Oh, say, can you see?

The future of this country?

It's cold,

people's hearts are warmed
with anger.

Anger at what changes us,

and what it shows as we watch
the events unfold.

It was the instigation that
hurts,

But should not surprise.

Those who do not learn from
history are doomed to repeat it.

Maybe the music didn't die
yet!

The more things change the
more they don't.

It’s been four years!

The talk is still toxic.

The hate rampant.

2020 was to be the year of diversity.

Instead, we got 250,000 Americans dead.

80 million dead worldwide.

Its 2021 now, we have three vaccines,

and another, million dead and counting.

The US Congress is writing
articles of Impeachment.

Again!

But this time they stormed the
capital.

like nobody could have seen
that coming.

Where were the troops?

Where was the Secret Service?

Why were there reporters,

But so, few to guard the peace?

History will judge the events of

Wednesday, January 6th, 2021.

So will a lot of other people.

All around the world,
People judge the United States,
by the actions of the President.

They change every four years.

The dance will begin again on

January 20th, 2021.

Let's hope the country will still exist in 2024.

The cure for what Ale's you

Things that are fermented
are supposed to be good,
for you.

Exercise strengthens muscles,
and twelve-ounce curls have
emboldened many an Armchair,
Quarterback.

Pickle juice has helped,
Many women make it through pregnancies.

Sour dough bread is Awesome!

But some of the things that have fermented:
Racial in justice,
Anti-Semitism,
Economic manipulation,
Hate
Political derision

And more?

They say Chicken soup and Kombucha

Can cure anything!

Sometimes

I wonder

Who “they” are.

Beauty fades, Stupid is forever!

Her hair has greyed,

but she has learned.

Her innovations have changed the world!

Time and time again.

She has powered the last two centuries,

and she has saved the human race.

She feeds everyone.

and still has bounty to spare!

However, times have changed!

A pandemic as wounded her like never before!

Food has been plowed under

because no one can leave their homes,

fires have ripped away her trees,

The heat of the planet is boiling her waters and killing the fish.

Yet action is being taken.

Millions of her children have died,

yet she has brought the survivors home.

Those in power have tried

and failed because the leader doesn't see it.

People have tried to remove him.

But he's still around.

Days may pass

Things may change.

But the damage is done.

She will recover

But at what cost?

I guess it's true what they say:

Beauty fades,

But stupid is forever!

Poetry is for people who

find themselves in strange places.

I've zoomed around the world now

several times over.

I've seen magnificent oceans

Majestic Peaks

Dreamy Skies

Powerful rivers

and the wonders of the cosmos

and all, without leaving my house!

Isn't technology amazing?

Snow

Life drifts in the changing winds

clean air chills as the temperature

changes.

Water comprises ninety-percent

of the planet earth

Heat evaporates water

and takes energy into being

White light

Contains all colors

Water flows in crystals

Drop by drop it flakes on to the grass.

Wow!

It happened!
The transition was peaceful!
And now sanity has returned to
the world.

But
Those who don't learn the
lessons of history are doomed
to repeat them.

The new President signed
fifteen new "Executive
orders."

Laws passed with the stroke of a pen can be unmade the same way.

He now has four years to get congress to enact legislation that will make those orders stick.

Otherwise

His successor can eliminate them or keep them at his/her Whim.

The was a poet or two at the event.

They sang and read with passion

And hope for the future.

The official poet
A Poet Laureate at twenty- two
Blows the mind of a nation
with her call to look for the
future.

Her challenge will mark
success or failure for the new
administration.

Will they find the pearls in her
wisdom?

Time will tell.

Sinking

Life is getting so busy
I'm learning a lot
but I'm losing sleep again.

Sometimes
one misses out
on the joys of life
because they are so occupied
with stuff that they forget.

Forget to be grateful
for being alive

for being loved

for having food to eat

for having a place to call home.

It's time to remember!

Remember to enjoy.

A rose

A kiss

A hug

A good conversation

And friendship.

Man the pumps!

I’m not drowning today!

I miss you

The time is passing

though it’s only been a few months

you were a big part of my life

You were fun to be with

most of the time

You had a special wisdom

That made me happy.

You taught me about

Heads

Shoulders

Knees

And toes

And helped me find out
Who stole the cookies
from the cookie jar.

Your children grew up without me.

I spent most of their lives in California

making my way through while
you raised them in

Maryland. We didn't see each
other for twenty years.

We reunited at your son's
wedding and it was like we
were never apart.

Covid-19 took you so
Myotonic Dystrophy couldn't

though it tried hard and almost
did.

Rest in peace.

I miss you!

Crystal Clear

For twenty years now
We've been running together

But

You've got another friend you
hang with now.

You say
they hate you
but you live with them.

Anything
I say is wrong now.
What happened?

You say you love me
and I love you too,
we've kept each other
Alive
and thriving during the time
we've known each other.

Now you want to surrender
To the demons
and give in.

Nothing I say can change your mind!

Maybe you need more than a friend.

Cody is a good puppy.

Maybe you need a different kind of love now.

I'm not giving up!

Sunflower 2

Touched by the gods
She carries her obsession
following her story
Through the folds of time
her tears feed her children
as they cover the earth in joy
Heartache leading to happiness
and the birth of a new season
And her name is Sunflower.

Musings 124

I’m really fortunate!
I’m alive!
I have my arms and legs
and they all work!

I have food to eat
and bills to pay,
most of them are paid right
now.

I can think!
Not everyone can say that at
this time.

There have been times
when I couldn't think!

When Ideas would flash
through my brain in eight
different languages and so fast
I couldn't tell which was
which!

My tongue has learned to
dance in American "English"
It had training wheels to learn
to ride Yiddish, Spanish,
French and "Brodspeak".

Romance has found me
and it is good.

Just a few musings for a
Sunday afternoon!

That’s the show

It’s done
The Earth shuttered
The Thunder roiled
The words were spoked.

The host was inexperienced
but the recording was clear.
Fortunately,
It was a “starter show”
and not that well known yet.

I got to advertise my books,

Even the collectors editions!
And mentioned a few of my
friends.

I came up with a few new
poems as samples
The recording copywrites them
as mine.
Somehow
an old tongue
got a workout
in a new format!
Poems can be found
everywhere!
Hallelujah!

Selma and the collar

"It's on inside out!"

"Yes, Selma."

I fix my shirt.

"You're such a good boychik.

All neat and clean.

You look so good and you help me so much!"

Yeah okay.

I need help getting dressed at 54.

But in my defense,

I do handle most of the grocery

shopping and get the mail most days.

9 car accidents and you still
say I help!

Physical injuries be dammed!

Well maybe,

Thanks for saying zo!

You are my Modrazine!

and I love you too!

84 years isn't enough!

Stick around a while.

I'll put on Mr. Tea Kettle

See you at 4:15 in the
morning!

www.ingramcontent.com/pod-product-compliance
Ingram Content Group UK Ltd.
Pitfield, Milton Keynes, MK11 3LW, UK
UKHW041347190726
13845UKWH00026B/474